This Is My Body:

Poems by a Teen Trans Fem

Madeline Aliah

This is My Body: Poems by a Teen Trans Fem
Copyright © Jamii Publishing 2023

Cover Art: Josie Lee O'Brien-Rojo

ISBN: 978-1-7332415-5-7

This Is My Body:

Poems by a Teen Trans Fem

I dedicate this book to my mother, Geneffa, the first ear to hear my poems and the first eye to review them. Your honesty and enthusiasm have shaped me and my writing.

I also dedicate this book to the little boy I used to be. You always wanted to become a writer. I hope you're proud of me.

Most of all, I dedicate this book to Cypress High School. Your diverse and accepting community is the hand on my shoulder as I discover who I truly am. You make me proud to be Trans.

Foreword

When I was eight years old, I decided I did not want to become a man. I had assumed that the moment I turned 18, my body would magically transform into a bearded monstrosity, and I resolved that dying was the preferable option.

I knew my disabled fingers were too clumsy to tie a noose, so I decided that the day I turned 18, I would find a way to get crushed by a giant bell. It's not like we learned about different ways to die at school, and this seemed quicker and flashier than being crucified like Jesus Christ.

As I grew up, manhood did not become any more appealing to me. I knew that trans people existed, but I had not been taught that this was anything more than a passing fad. Fortunately, I ended up at Cypress High School, which prides itself on inclusivity.

The Cypress community has given me many things, but the most important have been alternatives to suicide. I was afraid to transition at first. I had a lifetime of propaganda to shake off, and I had to make sure being a woman would be better for me than being a man.

I took it slow, and I can now say I am who I'm meant to be, and my life has never been better. I have found my people and my body. This community helped me realize how many options you have before ending your life.

I turn 18 this year, and when that day comes, instead of hunting down a giant bell, I will be waking up and going to school early.

This little book is an offering of 18 poems as candles for a birthday I didn't expect to reach. I hope it's a light for those who need it. I hope it helps the non-trans reader understand what it's like to be someone like me.

Most of all, I hope to build a kinder world for gender- queer kids like that little boy who would rather be crushed by a giant bell than turn into a man. I wish he had known there are better options for avoiding manhood. I am grateful he didn't know there are easier ways to die.

CONTENTS

THE BODY COUNTERFEIT

To

My Former Flesh

My god, how gracious I was to you.
I feel it in my lungs and brow.
How hard this fragile body fought!

I allowed you to grow
in a world of buried hatred
I can no longer tolerate.

Fall back into that soil.
Let me lay you to rest for real.
I am real.
You are not!

From

Someone Leaving

4

Ready

meat stretched along too much bone

skin stretched across too much meat

fabric stretched over too much skin

primed to explode

I Woke Up Twice This Morning

The first time I woke up this morning
I was an organ in my bed

A mouth hanging open
the words drowned out by involuntary breath

Muscles brace
the instinct to rise unrealized

To throw aside the covers
crawl out of my tomb
my shell
my can

To throw the window open and inhale
To step out my door in clothes that match my shape like they were
made for me

I see her in the doorway
and she is beautiful!

But like every other morning
I am forced to wake up twice.

The second time I wake up this morning
the bed's entrails spill onto the carpet

My mouth groans
ejecting the breath from my stomach

Muscles tense
and suddenly I am a rising body

drifting out the door
unable to congrue with my intention
my desire
my self

My second morning body is an oven
My first morning body is a dove

It simmers in the bathroom mirror and
disgusts me

Face Value

If I had a face
I would hold it in my hands
rest its jaw in my palms
feel their warmth on its cheeks
and remember what blushing feels like

If I had a face
I would trace my fingers over it
tickle my nose
caress my lips
and remember the crispness of deep breaths

If I had a face
I would show it to everyone
ruddy-cheeked and copper-eyed
smile at every pedestrian
and remember how to be human

If I had a face
I would stuff it with food
hotdogs, hamburgers
lick the grease off the plate
and remember to use my napkin

And if I had a face
I would take the sheet of skin that kept it
hidden
and nail it to the wall above my door

so passersby could see it
and remember to pay their respects

to the few hapless souls
left dreaming of what they'd do
if they had a face

This is my body

My body is a cyst
a rash
a hive
of roaches
that skitter and toil

My body is a basement
a ghetto
a culture
of cells
that excrete and embroil

My body is a growth
a rot
a mold
I do not
      fit in

Love me

Don't you love my new face?
Its teeth rattle in the wind
like flowers in a hurricane.
The noise tells you I love you.

Are you proud of my face?
The way its hair clumps fall out
like seed pods that sprout your name.
I pull them out for you.

Do you delight in my face?
The caves that form in its cheeks
cast waning sunset shadows.
Take comfort in their shelter.

Does my face bewitch you?
The way my new eyes glaze
not smiling
with my lips like you do.

Unusable

My mom
used to say
forgiving abusers allows closure—
hoping if it worked for me
it would for her

She also
used to say
my former self was her favorite child—
hoping I would understand
she loved me too

The boy in me
used to pretend
he was raping his inner woman
hoping it would make me
go away

If he can hear
I want that boy to know,

You got more love than you deserved.

I'm hoping that you never
come back.

THE BODY POLITIC

To
My Sweethearts in the Struggle,

My god, how grateful you make me
I feel it in my wrists and gut
How deep this righteous core rages

You coax me from
my little world of secret comfort
the rest would never allow

Take me in your arms.
Ground me with a cause that's real
Just like me
Just like us

From
Someone Yearning

Passed

Was it the long-haired boy
     I passed at nine
          that made me grow out mine?

Some iPhone meme
     I passed at twelve
          into which psychologists delve?

Did the rainbow flag
     I passed at fifteen
          turn me into a drag queen?

Then why, oh why
     did I at eight
          plan to be called the late?

Dear History

What would I give to be seen?

All the money in the world
if the hands of ghosts could hold purses

My facial facade
if it could exist in a vacuum

All the beauty I could muster
if transparent bodies caught on cameras

My body, for you
if I had one to give

My story, in full
and I have such a story to tell

But though dead women do tell tales,
dead men tell theirs louder

The Pronoun Game

She/Her/Hers
are dangerous pronouns to choose
because choosing them makes you dangerous.

She can walk into a woman's bathroom
and be surrounded by people with uteruses.
She could forget to wash her hands
or rape someone.

He/Him/His
are dangerous pronouns to choose
because choosing them makes you dangerous.

He can walk into a school
and be seen by a curious child.
He could use the wrong water fountain
or shoot someone.

They/Them/Theirs
are dangerous pronouns to choose
because choosing them makes you dangerous.

They can use the grammar wrong
and claim it's their right.
They could hold a rainbow rally
or start a riot.

I/Me/Mine
are dangerous pronouns to choose
because choosing me makes me dangerous.

I can see through the lie
of freedom being "not worth the risk."
I could choose to be free anyway
or kill myself.

First Trans Shooting

This poem is in memoriam of the 2023 Nashville shooting by Aiden Hale, and how it has been weaponized.

we are different

we are better

we are afraid

for our

lives

because monsters

will hate us,

undeserving

but now

I say this

you say that

neither listen

we were different

we were better

we got to fear

for our lives

and took for granted

the protection

pity provides

but now

this shoots that

that shoots this

both shoot children

Turncoats

I chose to be a man
Another rape is on the news
In a world
full of flaunting girls
I chose to be a man
To throw off the bra
and don the binder
To think of what really matters
and ask Google
if anything does
The door is closed
Another slash

Being a girl isn't easy
Look at them
Look around
It's hell out there
The Judge blamed the woman
The news says she thought she was alone
The night couldn't camouflage her skin
Unanimous Jury
A Bloodstain on my desk

Age 9 was "Just sad"
Age 11 was Tomboy"
Age 13 was "Emo"

Age 15 is "Selfish"
The woman on TV calls
for all girls far and wide
to stand together
Bloody fingers can't pause the video
they just leave a stain over the face
"Selfish"
"Selfish"
"Selfish"
Slash
Cut
Slice

I hear it every time
"How could you?"
"How can you leave us all behind?" "Us girls need you!"
"We are bleeding!" "We are starving!"
"Our wrists are bruised and you're leaving us all behind!"
The skin of my wrists is no longer visible

The room is spinning
I find the strength to turn my phone off
A part of me is glad I'm blacking out
I don't want to be awake
I don't want to feel pain
but neither do they
and I abandoned them

I fight to stay awake
because life hurts
and selfish men like me get what we deserve

I chose to be a woman
Another rape is on the news
In a world
full of flexing boys
I chose to be a woman
To shave away the facial hair
and don the bra
To think of what really matters
and ask Google
if anything does
The door is closed
Another thud

Being a girl isn't easy
Look at them
Look around
It's hell out there
The Judge blamed the woman
The news says she thought she was alone
The night couldn't camouflage her skin
Unanimous Jury
My head thuds against the wall

Age 9 was "Sensitive"
Age 11 was "Late bloomer"
Age 13 was "Queer"
Age 15 is "Arrogant"
The woman on TV calls
for all girls far and wide
to stand together
My head hits the wall again

this time my vision blurs
"Arrogant"
"Arrogant"
"Arrogant"
Bang
Slam
Thud

I hear it every time
"How could you?"
"How can you take this from us?"
"Womanhood is a gift!"
"Womanhood is an art!"
"We suffer, and we turn it into beauty!"
"It is the only thing we have, and you are taking it from us!"

That one was a crunch.
My vision is red
I am crumpling to the ground
A part of me is glad I'm blacking out
I don't want to be awake
I don't want to feel pain
but neither do they
and I'm robbing them

I fight to stay awake
because life hurts
and arrogant boys like me get what we deserve

Blood Sisters

*This poem is dedicated to the gay men who died during
the AIDS epidemic, and the Blood Sisters who gave
selflessly to fight it.*[1]

GLBT
Gay, Lesbian, Bisexual, Trans
Gays come first,
of course they do
Gay is male
Male is better
and they know it

HIV
Human Immunodeficiency Virus
(also faggot cancer)
Gays get it the most
everyone is scared
Nobody is safe
and they know it

MSM
Men who have Sex with Men
It's the official term
for people doctors refuse to treat
MSM is blood poison
MSM is poisoned blood
and they know it

---

[1]The acronym for Queer people was originally GLBT. However, the Blood Sisters and
other lesbian groups supporting their gay brothers during the AIDS epidemic
contributed to the placement of L first (Yale University Library).

BLOOD SISTERS
Dykes who volunteer where doctors resign
When no one will donate blood
they fill tanks and bags and fridges
to give to the ailing
Discrimination is a killer
and they know it.

LGBT
Lesbian, Gay, Bisexual, Trans
Ladies first
When their kin scorned them
they chose to show love
Love wins thanks to them
Yet we've forgotten, one by one

THE BODY MANIFEST

To

My Darling Self,

My god, how I love you
I feel it in my cheeks and chest.
How deep this newborn heart aches.

You coax me from
my little world of secret pain
the rest would never believe.

Take me in your arms.
Ground me in a place where this is real.
I am Real.
We are real.

From

Someone Grappling

The First Time

Small as a pinkie nail
white like a precious pearl
I still remember it

One of thirty pills
all of them alike
it would be the first

Placed on my desk
shone under light
every angle

Nothing will
be the same
after this

It's pinched
between
fingers

Here
We
Go

Trans Risk

0.5mg - white
1mg - pink
2mg - blue

It's a trans flag
With each dose, the trans risk rises
they warn me
brain strokes
breast cancers
blood clots
but I don't see a trans risk

I see a stroke of luck
that I lived this long

I see cancer in breasts
because I have them

I see the clot
of women gathering
in the arteries of your system

Does it bother you
that womanhood is a gift
worth dying for?

You Chose This

Head heavy, brain bowed
by the weight of what you've done
to yourself

You rejected the body you wanted
for something you could keep

Head bowed, brain heavy
with the weight of what you've done
for yourself

You traded the body you hated
for something you could lose

Soul Hunt

When you look to the future
      but can't see a thing

When you cling to your body
      but get pushed away

When you wake up in a world
      that considers you dead

When your layers peel apart
      faster than they grow

You find a presence
      you don't recognize at first

That insists you are more
      than the ways you bleed

Trans Maiden Manifesto

You saw a weak boy
     I was a smart girl
You saw a timid boy
     I was a gentle girl
You saw a pathetic boy
     I was a marvelous girl

You see a mad man
     I am a sad woman
You see a broken man
     I am a token woman
You see a disgusting man
     I am a distinguished woman

You might see an old lad
     I will be a bold lady
You might see a bitter lad
     I will be a savage lady
You might see a burdensome lad
     I will be a breathtaking lady

Look at you
     heart race
     hand sweat
     cheek flush
     blood rush
Look at her
     head tilted
     hair messy

grin impish
posture proud
She'll be there
through the window
at the puddle
on the phone screen
in the mirror
And she loves you
You love her
You are her and damn,
is she fine!

Who is the prettiest princess?

You

It's not a poem

It's a fact

Acknowledgments

Madeline thanks the following organizations for recognizing and publishing her work:

"Dear History," "Passed," "Soul Hunt," and "Trans Maiden Manifesto" were exhibited at the Santa Cruz County Government Office. 2023 Santa Cruz Parks Spotlight Award.

"Turncoats," *Journal X* (3rd ed.) 2023.

"Turncoats" was digitally published by *Mad in America*, "Beyond Labels and Meds–Closer Look: Madeline Aliah." (Feb. 28, 2023).

42

Volcanic Interruptions
by Adela Najarro
and Janet Trenchard

Soundcheck
by Elisa Grajeda-Urmston
and Tamara Adams

Sirens in Her Belly
by Romaine Washington

Expansions
by Micah Tasaka

Soul Sister Revue:
A Poetry Compilation
by Cynthia Manick

Gathering the Waters
by Keisha-Gaye Anderson

Maroon
by Angela Peñaredondo

Sarankara Collage
by Madonna Lavon Camel

Jamii is community. At Jamii Publishing we believe that poetry is not a solitary art.
Poetry is an art form that brings people together.
www.jamiipublishing.com
Jamii Publishing is a 501(c)(3) Charitable Organization

Made in the USA
Columbia, SC
24 August 2024

41109544R00030